ULTIMATE CAR BATTLES

BMW vs. MERCEDES

Colin Crum

WINDMILL
BOOKS
New York

Published in 2014 by Windmill Books, An Imprint of Rosen Publishing
29 East 21st Street, New York, NY 10010

First Edition

Produced for Windmill by Cyan Candy, LLC
Designer: Erica Clendening, Cyan Candy
Editor for Windmill: Joshua Shadowens

Photo Credits: Cover (top) Rob Wilson/Shutterstock.com; Cover (bottom), 8 Gustavo Fadel/
Shutterstock.com; pp. 4, 15 Darren Brode/Shutterstock.com; p. 5 Stefan Ataman/ Shutterstock.
com; p. 6 Ajtnk, via Wikimedia Commons; p. 7 Gyuszko-Photo/Shutterstock.com; p. 9
olgaru79/Shutterstock.com; p. 10 Dezidor, via Wikimedia Commons; p. 11 Lothar Spurzem,
via Wikimedia Commons; p. 12 Rudolf Stricker, via Wikimedia Commons; p. 13 Elena
Dijour/Shutterstock.com; p. 14 Stefan Krause, Germany, via Wikimedia Commons; p. 16 Art
Konovalov/Shutterstock.com; p. 17 hin255/Shutterstock.com; p. 18 Mihai Maxim/Shutterstock.
com; p. 19 cancer741 / Shutterstock.com; p. 20 MrSegui/Shutterstock.com; p. 21 David
Acosta Allely/Shutterstock.com; p. 22 M. Trischler, via Wikimedia Commons; p. 23 Ngchikit,
via Wikimedia Commons; p. 24 Dongliu/Shutterstock.com; p. 25 Patrick Poendl/Shutterstock.
com; p. 26 PhotoStock10/Shutterstock.com; p. 27 Stefan Ataman/Shutterstock.com; p. 30 (top)
Jaromir Shutterstock.com; p. 30 (bottom) eans/Shutterstock.com.

Library of Congress Cataloging-in-Publication Data

Crum, Colin.
BMW vs. Mercedes / by Colin Crum. — First edition.
    pages cm — (Ultimate car battles)
Includes index.
ISBN 978-1-4777-9011-3 (library) — ISBN 978-1-4777-9012-0 (pbk.) —
ISBN 978-1-4777-9013-7 (6-pack)
1. BMW automobiles—Juvenile literature. 2. Mercedes automobile—Juvenile literature.
I. Title.
TL215.B25C78 2014
629.222'2—dc23
                              2013022174

Manufactured in the United States of America

CPSIA Compliance Information: Batch #BW14WM: For Further Information contact Windmill Books, New York, New York at 1-866-478-0556

TABLE OF CONTENTS

CONSTANT COMPETITION

BMW and Mercedes-Benz are two German car companies. They are both known for making luxury vehicles. Luxury vehicles are meant to be beautiful, comfortable, and fast. They also have design and technology features that less expensive cars do not have. These features range from leather seats to **voice-recognition** systems. In 2012, BMW and Mercedes-Benz were the top two sellers of luxury vehicles in the United States.

BMW 135i Coupe

BMW introduced its first car with a V12 engine in 1995. This was the 750iL, powered by a 5.4-liter V12 engine. Mercedes-Benz followed up with the S600 and its 5.5-liter V12 engine in 1999.

BMW and Mercedes-Benz have a famous rivalry. Since they both make luxury cars, they must compete for customers. This means they are always trying to outdo each other with their many car models. For example, the Mercedes-Benz C-Class competes against the BMW 3 Series, and the BMW 5 Series competes against the Mercedes-Benz E-Class. Car fans love to argue about which company makes the ultimate luxury car!

ALL ABOUT BMW

BMW stands for Bayerische Motoren Werke. In English, this means Bavarian Motor Works. The BMW Auto Group's **headquarters** is in Munich, Germany. BMW is known for making its own luxury cars and motorcycles.

However, the BMW Auto Group also owns the companies that make Rolls-Royce and Mini cars.

BMW makes many different series, or classes, of vehicles. Models in these series have a range of body styles,

This is a Rolls-Royce Phantom. Rolls-Royce Motor Cars started as a British company called Roll-Royce Limited in 1906. The BMW Auto Group bought Rolls-Royce in 1998.

including coupes, convertibles, crossover SUVs, sedans, and roadsters. BMW's best-selling car is the 3 Series compact car. The 3 Series has been on Car and Driver's 10Best List more years in a row than any other car in the world!

The BMW Logo

The BMW logo is a circle divided into blue and white quarters. Some people think the logo is meant to look like a white airplane propeller against a blue sky. Other people think the logo is designed after the blue and white flag of Bavaria, the German state where BMW was started.

WHAT MAKES A MERCEDES-BENZ?

Mercedes-Benz is a division of Daimler Auto Group. Their headquarters is in Stuttgart, Germany. Mercedes-Benz is best known for making a range of luxury cars. However, they also make trucks and buses. Mercedes-Benz has been making luxury vehicles for more than 100 years!

Mercedes-Benz has always been famous for making **innovations** in **engineering**. For example, the 1909 Lightning Benz had a 21.5-liter engine that helped it set a

Mercedes-Benz Logo

This Mercedes-Benz 300 SC coupe was made in the late 1950s. You can see old Mercedes-Benz car models like this one at classic car shows around the world!

speed record at 124 miles per hour (200 km/h)! In 1978, Mercedes-Benz introduced their Antilock Braking System, which keeps steering wheels from locking up. In 2014, the E-Class uses **radar** technology to help drivers

The Mercedes-Benz Logo

The Mercedes-Benz logo is a three-pointed star inside a circle. The star was designed by Gottlieb Daimler in 1909. Each point on the star stands for a mode of transportation, or a way people can travel. These three modes are by air, by sea, or by land.

BMW'S BEGINNINGS

BMW did not start as a car company. In fact, in 1913, the company that would become BMW made aircraft engines!

However, after World War I, Germany no longer needed as many aircraft engines. In fact, many factories that

During World War II, BMW started making engines for German military aircraft again. They made 28,000 BMW 801 engines, such as the one shown here, during the war.

Přídi stíhacího letounu Focke-Wulf 190A
Přední část německého stíhacího letounu, který byl po druhé světové válce nalezena na našem území.
V přídi je zamontován dvouhvězdicový, vzduchem chlazený motor BMW 801 o výkonu 1250 kW (1700 k).
Motor je umístěn do původního montážního vozíku, který usnadňoval jeho instalaci do letounu.

Nose part of Focke-Wulf 190A fighter plane
The front part of a German fighter plane which was discovered on our territory after World War II. The front part is fitted with a double-row radial air-cooled engine BMW 801 with engine power 1250 kW (1700 k). The engine is mounted on an original assembly truck which facilitated its installation in the plane.

Motor / Engine	BMW 801 (1250 kW / 1700 HP)
Rozpětí / Wingspan	10,50 m
Délka / Length	8,95 m
Hmotnost prázdného letounu / Empty weight	2845 kg
Vzletová hmotnost / Take off weight	3995 kg
Maximální rychlost / Max. speed	673 km/h
Dostup / Service ceiling	10 600 m / 800 km

The BMW 328, shown here, had a roadster body style. Roadsters are open-topped cars with just two seats. Just 464 BMW 328s were built between 1936 and 1940!

made aircraft parts had to shut down. Instead, BMW switched to making engines and other parts for boats, cars, trucks, and motorcycles. In 1929, BMW sold its first car, the BMW 3/15 DA-2. This car had a top speed of just 45 miles per hour (75 km/h)!

One of BMW's early models is also one of the most famous sports cars of all time! BMW introduced the 328 sports car in 1936. The 328 won more than 120 races between 1936 and 1940. In 1954, BMW built its first car with a V8 engine, the 502.

THE START OF MERCEDES-BENZ

The Mercedes-Benz name came from the **merger** of two different companies. The first company was started by Karl Benz. Benz patented the first petrol-powered car in 1886. The second company was started by Gottlieb Daimler and Wilhelm Maybach. The Daimler company started selling Mercedes cars in 1901. In 1926, Daimler-Benz was founded. They started selling the first Mercedes-Benz cars the same year.

This is a Mercedes-Benz 770 Series II cabriolet. Cabriolets are cars with fold-down roofs. The 770 Series II cars were built between 1938 and 1943.

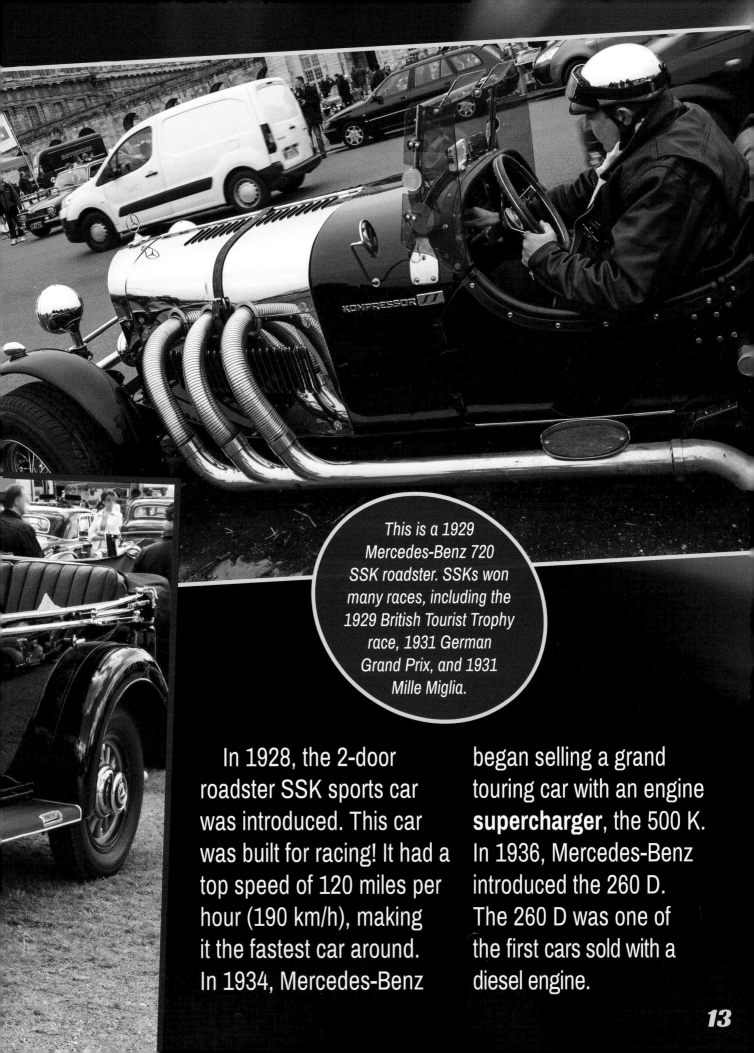

This is a 1929 Mercedes-Benz 720 SSK roadster. SSKs won many races, including the 1929 British Tourist Trophy race, 1931 German Grand Prix, and 1931 Mille Miglia.

In 1928, the 2-door roadster SSK sports car was introduced. This car was built for racing! It had a top speed of 120 miles per hour (190 km/h), making it the fastest car around. In 1934, Mercedes-Benz began selling a grand touring car with an engine **supercharger**, the 500 K. In 1936, Mercedes-Benz introduced the 260 D. The 260 D was one of the first cars sold with a diesel engine.

CHANGES FOR BMW

In the 1950s, BMW was having money problems. Their 507 roadster was a beautiful car, but it was too expensive. In 1959, the company almost got taken over by their rival, Daimler-Benz! However, in the 1960s, BMW introduced their New Class cars. These popular models sold very well. The 1500 was a 4-cylinder sports car introduced in 1961. It was soon followed by the more powerful and fast 1800

BMW 507 Roadster

Isetta Microcar

*In 1955, BMW started selling BMW Isetta microcars. These cars were nicknamed "bubble cars" because of their shape. The 1955 BMW Isetta 250 was powered by a 12-**horsepower**, or HP, motorcycle engine. Later models included the 300 and the 600. Between 1955 and 1962, BMW sold more than 161,000 Isettas!*

in 1964. The 2002, a two-door sedan, was introduced in 1968.

In the 1970s, BMW launched their 3 Series, 5 Series, and 7 Series models. These cars have been redesigned many times, but they are still being sold today!

MERCEDES-BENZ OVER TIME

In 1954, Mercedes-Benz introduced one of their most well-known models, the 300SL. This lightweight two-seater sports car was famous for its gull-wing door design and top speed of 155 miles per hour (250 km/h). The 300SL was also the start of the Mercedes-Benz SL-Class, which have now gone through six **generations** of designs!

The 1961, Mercedes-Benz introduced their "fintail" models, which had tail fins to improve the cars'

Mercedes-Benz 300SL

This is a 1957 Mercedes-Benz 190SL. This 2-door roadster could be bought with a hardtop convertible roof. The 190SLs were made between 1955 and 1963.

aerodynamics. The New Generation Models of sedans and coupes were launched in 1968.

These cars were known for their square lines. By the 1990s, Mercedes-Benz was making A-Class, C-Class, CLK-Class, SL-Class, and E-Class models.

C111 Research Car

Mercedes-Benz introduced the C111 **concept car** at the Frankfurt International Motor Show in 1969. This superfast car had a futuristic fiberglass body. Mercedes-Benz used the C111 model as a research car in the 1970s to experiment with new engines. These included Wankel rotary engines and powerful turbodiesel engines.

BMW IN RACING

BMW has a long history in motorsports. Before World War II, BMW motorcycles competed in racing. In 1939, Georg Meier won the Isle of Man TT riding a BMW motorcycle. BMW motorcycles continue to race and win today!

BMW has also been very successful in sports car and touring car racing. Their wins include the 24 Hours of Daytona, American Le Mans Series, and the European Tour Car Championships. The BMW Motorsport division

Here, Hungarian driver Nikolett Szanto races in her BMW Z4 at the 2011 Drift Grand Prix of Romania. Before driving the Z4, Szanto raced with a BMW E36.

This is the BMW V12 LMR racing car built by BMW Motorsport. This car is famous for BMW's first overall win in the 1999 24 Hours of Le Mans.

has developed many BMW racecars, including the 1972 BMW 3.0 CSL, the 1980 BMW M1, and the 1996 McLaren F1 GTR. In 1999, the BMW V12 LMR won the 24 Hours of Le Mans race.

BMW-powered cars won 20 Formula 1 races between 1950 and 2009, including a 1983 Driver Championship and 20 Grand Prix wins. BMW competed as the BMW Sauber team between 2006 and 2009.

MERCEDES-BENZ IN RACING

Mercedes-Benz also has a long history in racing. In the 1930s, Mercedes-Benz Silver Arrows competed in Grand Prix racing with many wins. The W196R racecar won Formula One world championship titles for Mercedes-Benz in 1954 and 1955, and a 300 SLR won the 1955 Mille Miglia endurance race.

After a terrible accident caused by a Mercedes-Benz driver at the 1955 24 Hours of Le Mans race, the company did not take part in racing for many years. However, private teams continued to

2013 Mercedes F1 W04

Here, Lewis Hamilton of the Mercedes AMG Petronas F1 Team gets ready for a training session. The 2013 Mercedes F1 team races with the Mercedes F1 W04.

drive Mercedes-Benz racing cars, such as the W111, the C/R 107, the W115/114, the W113, and the G Model.

In the 1990s, Mercedes-Benz built engines for the Sauber and McLaren Formula One teams. They returned to Formula One with their own team in 2010. Today, Mercedes-Benz also competes in Formula Three and DTM racing.

GOING HEAD-TO-HEAD

One place Mercedes-Benz and BMW racing cars compete head-to-head is the DTM racing series. In English, DTM stands for German Touring Car Masters. Mercedes-Benz has taken part in DTM racing since it started in 2000. Since 2000, Mercedes-Benz has won 6 championships for their cars and 9 championships for their drivers. BMW joined the DTM series in 2012. They won both the car and driver championships in their first year.

This is a Mercedes-Benz C-Class car used for DTM racing. The Mercedes AMG DTM team competed with this car in the 2006 DTM season.

Here, a driver from BMW Team Schnitzer races in a BMW M3 GT2. This car won the 2010 Intercontinental Le Mans Cup in Zhuhai, China.

In 2013, Mercedes-Benz had two teams competing in the DTM series. These teams drove Mercedes-Benz C-Coupes. BMW competed in the DTM with four teams. These teams raced driving BMW M3s.

24 Hours Nürburgring

Mercedes-Benz and BMW also went head-to-head in the 41st 24 Hours Nürburgring endurance race in May 2013. A Mercedes-Benz SLS AMG GT3 won the race, finishing just ahead of a BMW Z4 GT3. This was Mercedes-Benz's first overall win at the 24 Hours Nürburgring. However, BMW racecars have won the race 19 times since 1970!

BMW NOW

Today, BMW is still competing with Mercedes-Benz to be the top-selling luxury carmaker in the world. BMW offers many different car series in a range of body styles. These include luxury and high-performance coupes, sedans, convertibles, roadsters, and crossover SUVs. Many models are also available with BMW's ActiveHybrid technology, which combines BMW engines with electric motors and lithium-ion high-performance batteries.

This is the BMW Vision ConnectedDrive concept car shown at the 2011 Geneva Auto Show. This car used different colored lights to show off BMW's ideas for new technologies.

Here, the BMW i8 concept car is shown at the 2011 Frankfurt Motor Show. This plug-in hybrid electric sports car was put into production for 2013.

BMW is also working on several concept cars. The X4 concept combines the BMW X crossover SUV idea with the sportiness of a coupe. The Active Tourer is concept for a luxury compact that would use electric driving technology but still perform like a BMW.

Concept 4 Series Coupe

BMW's 4 Series Coupe is an example of a concept car that was put in production. In 2012, BMW introduced the model as a concept for BMW coupe with long lines, a low roof, and a sporty look. In late 2013, 4 Series coupes and convertibles became available to buyers.

MERCEDES-BENZ TODAY

Today, Mercedes-Benz offers a wide-range of luxury car and SUV classes in many different body styles. Their most popular cars are the C-Class sedans and coupes. Their fastest, most powerful models are the high-performance roadsters and supercars designed by AMG.

What is next for Mercedes-Benz? In 2014, Mercedes-Benz is introducing their B-Class Electric Drive model.

The Mercedes-Benz A-Class concept vehicle was introduced at the 2011 New York Auto Show. The A-Class concept is a 3-door hatchback built to compete with the BMW 1 Series.

Concept A-CLASS.

Here, the Mercedes SLS AMG Coupe Electric Drive is shown at the 2012 Paris Auto Show. This car's gullwing doors and a liquid blue paint finish caught many people's eyes!

This compact battery-powered car can still reach a top speed of 100 miles per hour (160 km/h)! They are also offering eye-catching redesigned 2014 S-Class sedans and 2014 E-Class coupes and cabriolets. The special 2014 C63 AMG 507 Edition can make 507 HP with its 6.2-liter V8 engine!

2014 SLS AMG Black Series

The 2014 SLS AMG Black Series is a special limited edition version of the SLS AMG Coupe. The design of this car is inspired by the SLS AMG GT3 racecar. It has gullwing doors, a front splitter, carbon-fiber trim, and a rear-spoiler. This car will go from 0 to 60 miles per hour (0–97 km/h) in under 3.5 seconds!

SIDE-BY-SIDE

BMW and Mercedes-Benz are both battling to be the best luxury carmaker. Car fans love to argue about which company is better.

BMW

Date Founded	**1916**
First Model	**1929 BMW 3/15 PS DA 2**
Current Owner	**BMW Auto Group**
Headquarters	**Munich, Germany**
Current Models in 2013–2014	**1 Series** **2 Series** **3 Series** **4 Series** **5 Series** **6 Series** **7 Series** **X1** **X3** **X5** **X6** **Z4** **M Models (M3, M4, M5, M6, X5 M, X6 M)**
Best 0–60 mph (0–97 km/h)	**2013 BMW M6 Coupe 4.1 seconds**
Most Powerful Engine	**2013 BMW M5 4.4L Turbocharged V8, 560 HP**
Best-Selling Model	**3 Series**
Cars Sold in the US, 2012	**281,460**

One way to decide between BMW and Mercedes-Benz cars is to **compare** the companies side-by-side. This chart will help you compare BMW with Mercedes-Benz!

MERCEDES-BENZ

Date Founded	1926
First Model	1926 Mercedes-Benz Model K
Current Owner	Daimler Auto Group
Headquarters	Stuttgart, Germany
Current Models in 2013–2014	C-Class CL-Class CLS-Class E-Class G-Class GL-Class GLK-Class M-Class S-Class SL-Class SLK-Class SLS-Class AMG Models (45, 55, 63, 65)
Best 0–60 mph (0–97 km/h)	2014 Mercedes-Benz SLS AMG Black Series 3.5 seconds
Most Powerful Engine	2010 Mercedes-Benz SL 65 AMG Black Series 6 Twin-Turbocharged V12, 660 HP
Best-Selling Model	C-Class
Cars Sold in the US, 2012	274,134

YOU DECIDE!

BMW and Mercedes-Benz are the top two luxury car companies in the world. They are known for making beautiful, comfortable cars with extra features that car fans love! Each year, BMW and Mercedes-Benz battle with each other to sell the most cars. Because of this, both push themselves to create new technologies and exciting designs.

Some people prefer BMWs. Others like Mercedes-Benz better. In the racing world, both companies have fans. However, only you can decide which company makes the best luxury car!

2013 Mercedes-Benz SL65 AMG

BMW Concept Spyder i8

GLOSSARY

aerodynamics (er-oh-dy-NA-miks) The study of ways to make things move through the air easily.

compare (kum-PER) To see how two or more things are alike or unlike.

concept car (KON-sept KAR) A car to show new features and technology.

engineering (en-juh-NIR-ing) The work that uses scientific knowledge for practical things, such as designing machines.

generations (jeh-nuh-RAY-shunz) Things made during the same period.

headquarters (HED-kwor-turz) A center of operations where leaders work and give orders.

horsepower (HORS-pow-ur) The way an engine's power is measured. One horsepower is the power to lift 550 pounds (250 kg) 1 foot (.3 m) in 1 second.

innovations (ih-nuh-VAY-shunz) Creating new things.

merger (MER-jur) The combination of two or more things, especially businesses, into one.

radar (RAY-dar) A machine that uses sound waves or radio waves to locate objects.

supercharger (SOO-pur-char-jur) An air compressor used to increase the pressure, temperature, and density of air supplied to an internal combustion engine.

voice-recognition (VOYS reh-kug-NIH-shun) Technology that allows your voice to control certain parts of a machine.

FURTHER READING

Adler, Dennis. *Mercedes-Benz*. Minneapolis, MN: MBI Publishing Company, 2008.

Colson, Rob Scott. *BMW*. Ultimate Cars. New York: PowerKids Press, 2010.

Hammond, Richard. *Car Science*. New York: DK Publishing, 2008.

INDEX